Dinosaurs

Preschool/Kindergarten

Save time and energy planning thematic units with this comprehensive resource. We've searched through the 1990–1997 issues of **The MAILBOX**® and **Teacher's Helper**® magazines to find the best ideas for you to use when teaching a thematic unit on dinosaurs. Included in this book are favorite units from the magazines, single ideas to extend a unit, and a variety of reproducible activities. Pick and choose from these activities to develop your own complete unit or simply to enhance your current lesson plans. You're sure to find everything you need right here in this book to create an integrated unit that's larger than life!

Editors:
Michele M. Dare
Angie Kutzer

Artists:
Teresa R. Davidson
Kimberly Richard

Cover Artist:
Kimberly Richard

www.themailbox.com

©1999 by THE EDUCATION CENTER, INC.
All rights reserved.
ISBN# 1-56234-322-X

Manufactured in the United States
10 9 8 7 6 5 4

Table Of Contents

Thematic Units...

from The MAILBOX® magazine

A Prehistoric Preschool
Welcome

Rumble, rumble. Stomp, stomp, stomp! Could that be the sound of dinosaurs thundering down the hall? No, but it *could* be the sound of excited preschoolers arriving at your door! Calm your Jurassic jitters by using these dinosaur-themed ideas to prepare a prehistoric preschool welcome for your new class. Have a "tremenda-saurus" year!

ideas contributed by dayle timmons and Angie Kutzer

A Prehistoric Present For You!

You can have enormous impact on youngsters' entry into preschool with these pre-preschool fun packs. Before the first day of school, prepare a dinosaur project, a dinosaur nametag, a welcome note, and dinosaur crayons for each child. Then deliver the fun packs during home visits prior to opening day. To prepare a pack for each child, duplicate the dinosaur pattern on page 7 onto white construction paper, the note on page 8 onto colorful paper, and a dinosaur nametag on page 9 onto colorful construction paper; then cut them out. Personalize the dinosaur pattern and nametag. To make dinosaur crayons for each child, put old crayons of the same color in a microwave-safe dish. Microwave on low, stirring occasionally. Pour the melted crayon wax into dinosaur-shaped candy molds (available where cake and candy supplies are sold). Place the molds in the freezer; then pop out the crayon shapes when they're solid. Seal one of each color of crayon in a plastic sandwich bag. Place the dinosaur pattern, note, nametag, and crayons in a lunch bag decorated with dinosaur stickers or dinosaur-themed notepad pages. Later use youngsters' completed dinosaur projects during your first group time, as described in "Getting To Know 'You-asaurus' " on page 5.

These dinosaur paws are on the floor, so you can follow them to Mrs. Timmons' door!

Making Tracks

Encourage independence by creating a "dino-rific" path that your little foot stompers can follow to your class on the first days of school. Make a dinosaur-paw template by enlarging the pattern on page 8 to the desired size. Then trace a supply of the pattern onto colorful Con-Tact® covering. Cut out the paws; then attach them to the floor in a path that leads from the school entrance to your classroom door. If desired, post a sign near the beginning of the path that reads, "These dinosaur paws are on the floor, so you can follow them to [your name]'s door!" Parents and children alike will be making tracks to find out what else you have in store!

Rip-Roarin' Ready To Start The Day!

Once your little ones have arrived at your door, greet each one with a dinosaur hug. Assist each child in attaching the nametag that he received in his fun pack to his clothing; then guide him to your group area. To get youngsters ready to follow daily routines, read aloud *Time For School, Little Dinosaur* by Gail Herman (Random House, Inc.; 1990). After listing Little Dinosaur's steps for getting ready for school, ask volunteers to offer ways that they got ready to come to school that morning, such as brushing their teeth or helping to prepare their snacks. Explain that a routine is also necessary each day once they arrive at school. Demonstrate the routine you would like youngsters to follow that includes activities such as putting belongings in cubbies and choosing centers. Then have each child step out into the hall and reenter the classroom, pretending that he has just arrived. Before you know it, students will be rip-roarin' ready to start the day—just like Little Dinosaur!

Getting To Know "You-asaurus"

Use the *extinct* to discover the *distinct* personalities that make up your new class. Invite youngsters to bring their completed dinosaur projects (see "A Prehistoric Present For You!" on page 4) with them to one of your first group times. Compare the dinosaurs. Then, using the accompanying note as your guide, discuss the similarities and differences that the dinosaurs reveal about your children. Collect the dinosaurs and display them—along with an enlarged copy of the note—on a bulletin board that can easily be seen by parents as they visit your school. This class is "dino-mite"!

An Invitation To A Dinosaur Stomp!

The invitation's out to watch tails wag, scales shake, and horns hoot and holler in Paul Stickland's *Dinosaur Stomp!* (Dutton Children's Books, 1996). Don't miss your chance to read about the dinosaur dance. Then follow up the fun by doing "The Dino Dance-O." To prepare personalized puppets for your little ones to take out on the dance floor, duplicate a class supply of the dinosaur patterns on page 9 onto various colors of construction paper. Personalize each dinosaur with a different child's name, cut out the patterns, and then tape each one to a craft stick. After sharing the story, give each child his puppet and direct him to find his own space in an open area of your room. Encourage your little ones to boogie down with their dinos as you lead them in singing the following song. That's what it's all about!

The Dino Dance-O
(sung to the tune of "The Hokey-Pokey")

You put your dino up,
You put your dino down,
You put your dino up,
And you shake it all around.

You do the Dino Dance-O
And you turn yourself around.
Stomp twice on the ground.
Dino Dance-O!

You put your dino in front,
You put your dino in back,
You put your dino in front,
And you give your knees a slap.

(Repeat chorus.)

You touch your dino to your head,
You touch your dino to your toe,
You touch your dino to your head,
Then you shake it to and fro.

(Repeat chorus.)

You do the Dino Dance-O.
You do the Dino Dance-O.
You do the Dino Dance-O.
That's what it's all about.
Dino Dance-O!

Brontosaurus Behavior

Use the characteristics of two dinosaur opposites, brontosaurus and tyrannosaurus, to discuss appropriate classroom behavior with your little ones. Locate in reference books pictures of a brontosaurus and a tyrannosaurus. Looking at the pictures, have the children compare the dinosaurs' physical features and share any information that they may already know about the two types of dinosaurs. Explain that the tyrannosaurus is thought to have been a mean meat-eater, while the brontosaurus is thought to have been a gentle plant-eater. Make a list of your little ones' suggestions for classroom behaviors that are brontosaurus-like. Then make a list of tyrannosaurus-like behaviors to avoid. Post the lists in the classroom; then refer to them when a rambunctious reptile needs to be reminded to act more like a lovable lizard.

We share.
We say nice words.
We help.

"Tour-ific" Fossils

Introduce your students to their new surroundings and school staff by going on a dinosaur search. To prepare for this activity, enlarge a dinosaur pattern from page 9 onto a piece of poster board. Cut out the dinosaur; then cut it into as many puzzle pieces as there are places and people to visit on your school tour. "Hide" a dinosaur fossil (puzzle piece) at each tour stop, and give one to each person you will introduce to your children on the tour.

Before your dinosaur hunt, explain to your paleontologists that fossils can be the remains of animals that lived thousands or millions of years ago. Read aloud *Bones, Bones, Dinosaur Bones* by Byron Barton (HarperCollins Children's Books, 1990). Suggest that there may be dinosaur fossils throughout your school; then take the group on a dinosaur search. Each time the group finds a fossil, introduce them to the new person or place where the fossil was found. Then return to the classroom to put the fossils together to make the dinosaur. Keep the dinosaur fossils in a puzzle center for youngsters to use independently.

I'm A Preschool Paleontologist!

Chances are your preschoolers are feeling proud of their paleontologic efforts. Top off your day by making these dinosaur headbands. Duplicate a supply of the dinosaur patterns on page 9 onto various colors of construction paper. Cut out the patterns for younger preschoolers. To make a headband, a child chooses a number of the dinosaur patterns, cuts them out if necessary, and decorates them with markers. He then glues them to a personalized sentence strip. Staple the ends of each child's strip together to fit his head. Look at me! I'm as proud as can be!

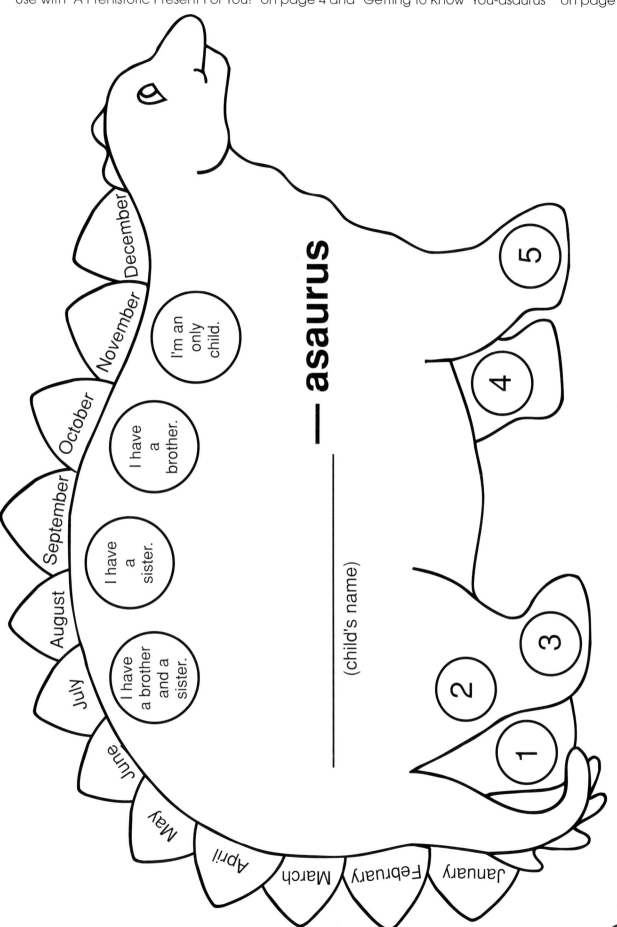

Note

Use with "A Prehistoric Present For You!" on page 4 and "Getting To Know 'You-asaurus'" on page 5.

Dear Preschool Pal,

You're big now—so stomp on down to preschool for a "dino-mite" time!

Color the dinosaur in your preschool fun pack. On the first day of school, bring the dinosaur and your nametag to school. Are you rip-roarin' ready? See you soon!

● How many years old are you? Color the same number of dots on the dinosaur's legs.

● When is your birthday? Color the dinosaur's spike that shows your birth month.

● Do you have a brother, a sister, both, or neither? Color the dot on the dinosaur's body.

● Color the dinosaur using your favorite color of crayon.

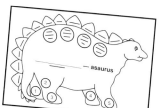

Dinosaur Paw Pattern

Use with "Making Tracks" on page 4.

8

Use with "A Prehistoric Present For You!" on page 4, "Rip-Roarin' Ready To Start The Day!" and "An Invitation To A Dinosaur Stomp!" on page 5, and "'Tour-ific' Fossils" and "I'm A Preschool Paleontologist!" on page 6.

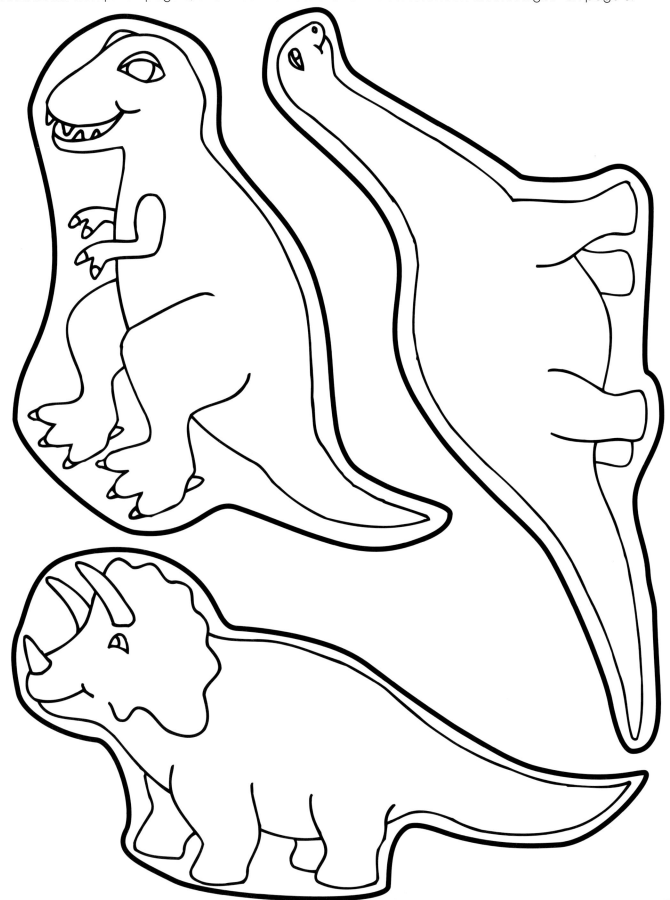

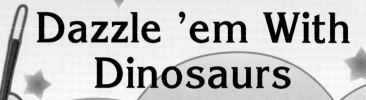

Dazzle 'em With Dinosaurs

ideas by Lucia Kemp Henry

Maybe it's that they were larger than life. Maybe it's that so much about them has been left to the imagination. But whatever the reasons, young children have an insatiable fascination with prehistoric creatures. Knowing this, we've packed five pages with top-notch dinosaur ideas. So, go ahead, razzle-dazzle 'em with reptiles from long, long ago.

Dinosaur Duds

Although fossilized bones give us a concrete model of dinosaurs' scaffoldings, our impressions of their outer coverings are largely theory-based. Read aloud the poem below to propel students into imaginative thoughts about the colors and textures of dinosaur hides. Discuss the poem and brainstorm with your youngsters lists of ideas for skin colors and textures.

As you are discussing textures, ask youngsters to observe interesting surface textures around the classroom. Give each youngster a white construction-paper copy of page 15, 16, or 17 and a crayon from which the paper has been removed. Have each child place his paper atop a textured surface, dinosaur pattern up, and make a crayon rubbing. Have students cut out these textured dinosaurs and display them on a black bulletin-board background with gray paper boulders, the largest of which bears a copy of "Decked-out Dinosaurs."

Too Big For Words

Help your youngsters imagine just how big dinosaurs were by using the chart supplied here. Have youngsters compare the sizes of several dinosaurs to common things such as trees, cars, buses, and buildings. Lead your youngsters in brainstorming synonyms for the word *big*. Then ask each student to write or dictate a sentence telling about the size of a dinosaur. Supply a length of bulletin board paper and paints, and have students take turns painting giant dinosaurs on the paper. When the artwork is dry, copy students' sentences into speech balloons drawn on the paper, so that the dinosaurs appear to be saying the sentences.

Ornitholestes	6 feet
Camptosaurus	15 feet
Stegosaurus	20 feet
Tyrannosaurus rex	40 feet
Apatosaurus	80 feet

Decked-out Dinosaurs

What kind of skin
Did a dinosaur wear?
Did it have some feathers?
Did it have some hair?

What were the colors
It wore in those days?
Were they bright reds and pinks
Or cool blues and grays?

How did it feel
To touch dinosaur skin?
Was it bumpy and thick
Or slick, smooth, and thin?

How do we know
What a dinosaur wore?
We imagine and color…
That's what crayons are for!

by Lucia Kemp Henry

A dinosaur was as big as my mom's car!

"Sculpt-asaurus"

Here's another hands-on opportunity for your youngsters to conjure up the dinosaurs in their imaginations and bring them into reality. Give each youngster ceramic clay or stiff baker's clay to sculpt into a dinosaur figurine. Fire, glaze, and refire the ceramic clay versions and bake, paint, and seal the baker's clay ones. Ask each student to create an original "scientific" name for his dinosaur. Create a tabletop exhibit by displaying each dinosaur with a name card.

Spikasaurus

Dino Laid An Egg
(to the tune of "This Old Man")

Verse 1 Di-no-saur
          She laid one.
          She laid one egg,
          Then was done.

Chorus Oh-oh, she lays dino eggs,
          Lays them one by one.
          She lays eggs until she's
             done!

Verse 2 Di-no-saur
          She laid two.
          She laid two eggs
          That were blue.

Repeat Chorus

Verse 3 Di-no-saur
          She laid three.
          She laid three eggs
          By a tree.

Repeat Chorus

Verse 4 Di-no-saur
          She laid four.
          She laid four eggs,
          Not one more.

Repeat Chorus

Verse 5 Di-no-saur
          She laid five.
          She laid five
          That hatched ALIVE!

Repeat Chorus

Counting Eggs

With this rousing rendition of "This Old Man" and the flannelboard patterns on page 18, your brood can have a great deal of counting, singing fun! Color and prepare the dinosaur and egg patterns for flannelboard use. Place the mother dinosaur at the top of the flannelboard and add (or have students add) the appropriate egg cutout as you sing each verse of the song. Be certain that the five-egg cutout is placed on the board with the hatchlings covered by eggshell tops. On the word "ALIVE!," remove the tops of the eggshells to reveal the hatchlings.

Egg Hunt

If you're having an Easter egg hunt this year, consider having a dinosaur egg hunt instead of a traditional one. You will need food coloring, 1" x 2" sponge pieces, empty egg cartons, plastic lids, and cooled, extra-large, hard-boiled chicken eggs. Put a few drops of a different color of food coloring on each of your lids. Press one end of a sponge in food coloring. Lightly sponge half of the egg for a mottled effect. Set the egg on an overturned egg carton bottom to dry. Repeat the sponging process later to complete the other egg half. When the egg is dry, overprint the first color with another color using the same sponging method. Once dried, your "dinosaur eggs" are ready for a great dinosaur egg hunt!

Festive Fieldwork

Create plenty of enthusiasm for your dinosaur egg hunt with these collection bags. To make a dinosaur egg hunt bag, cover one panel of a shopping bag with construction paper that has been cut to fit. Glue it in place. Cut out, color, and label a copy of the mother dinosaur on page 18. Glue the dinosaur cutout near the top of the bag panel. Then glue bits of construction paper, tissue paper, twigs, yarn, and string below her to create a nest. When you send your little ones off to collect dinosaur eggs in these bags, there's going to be a lot of festive fieldwork going on!

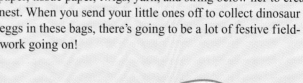

Kevin's Dino-Eggs

Dino Bingo

With our reproducible pieces, it's easy to make a dinosaur bingo game that your youngsters will delight in. On colored tagboard, reproduce the bingo card on page 19. On white construction paper, reproduce the bingo card pieces on page 20. Have each student cut out one set of card pieces and glue them randomly on his bingo card. Label footprint-shaped flash cards *1* through *8*.

Play the game by holding up a flash card. Students read the numeral, find the matching set of footprints on their cards, and mark their cards with small jelly bean "dinosaur eggs." The first person to have three dino eggs in a row in any direction wins.

"Lotto-saurus"

Prepare this lotto game for students to use independently. Reproduce the lotto patterns (page 21) on tagboard. Color the dinosaurs on the cards, one dinosaur to match each color indicated on the lotto gameboard. Color the artwork at the top of the lotto card as desired. Laminate before cutting out the cards and the lotto gameboard. Store the pieces in a Ziploc® bag that has been decorated with dinosaur stickers. To play, a student matches each dinosaur card to the matching word on the lotto gameboard.

Prehistoric Piñata

A giant papier-mâché dinosaur egg may be just what you've been looking for to perk up a party. Papier-mâché a large, inflated oval balloon. Leave an opening near the smaller end for filling the piñata. Reinforce a two-inch border around the opening with several extra layers of papier-mâché. Sponge paint the dry papier-mâché with several colors of bright paint. Remove the balloon, poke holes in the reinforced rim, and thread with yarn for hanging. Label a plastic bag with each student's name and fill it with dinosaur treats and jelly beans. Stuff the bags inside the piñata and suspend it from the ceiling. Give each youngster a turn to be blindfolded and whack at the piñata with a stick. Keep the remainder of the youngsters a safe distance away until the treats come spilling to the ground.

Glue And Crayon Rubbings

Little ones can have a big time with this dinosaur project. In advance, enlarge or trace dinosaur designs onto tagboard. Have student volunteers run a trail of glue atop each of the lines on the tagboard. Or, if you prefer to make these preparations, use a hot glue gun to run a trail of glue atop the lines. Allow the glue to dry thoroughly. Tape each prepared piece of tagboard to a tabletop. To create a crayon rubbing, a youngster selects the design of his choice, places a sheet of art paper on top of it, and rubs the paper with the side of a crayon until the dinosaur design appears.

Jennifer Strathdee—Pre-K Special Education
Parkside School
Auburn, NY

Enormously Popular T-Shirts

Children can do a marvelous job of creating dinosaur T-shirts with a little creative assistance from you! Iron Wonder Under® to a length of felt. Cut the felt into squares and have each youngster trace a dinosaur template onto a square. Cut out the dinosaurs, peel off the paper backing, and press each onto a T-shirt. Have students squeeze fabric paint around the perimeter of the design, if desired. Then stitch on a wiggle eye or use fabric paint to make an eye. Invite students to turn their shirts into original works of art by adding more fabric paint details.

adapted from an idea by Nina Tabanian—Pre-K
St. Bernard Of Clairvaux
Dallas, TX

Dinosaur Chow

Grins and giggles will abound as your youngsters stir up this tasty "dinosaur food." If desired, cover the labels of the ingredients with labels to match the ingredients list below.

Dinosaur Delight

1/4 cup dirt (cocoa)
1/2 cup swamp water (milk with green food coloring)
2 cups crushed bones (sugar)
1/2 cup fat (butter)
2 cups dead grass (uncooked oatmeal)
1/2 cup squashed bugs (peanut butter)

Mix dirt and swamp water. Add crushed bones and fat. Boil about 3 minutes. Add squashed bugs and dead grass, and stir until melted. Remove from heat and stir until mixture begins to thicken. Drop by tablespoonfuls onto waxed paper. Cool, eat, and enjoy!

Sheila Brossmann—Pre-K
Wallis Elementary School
Wallis, TX

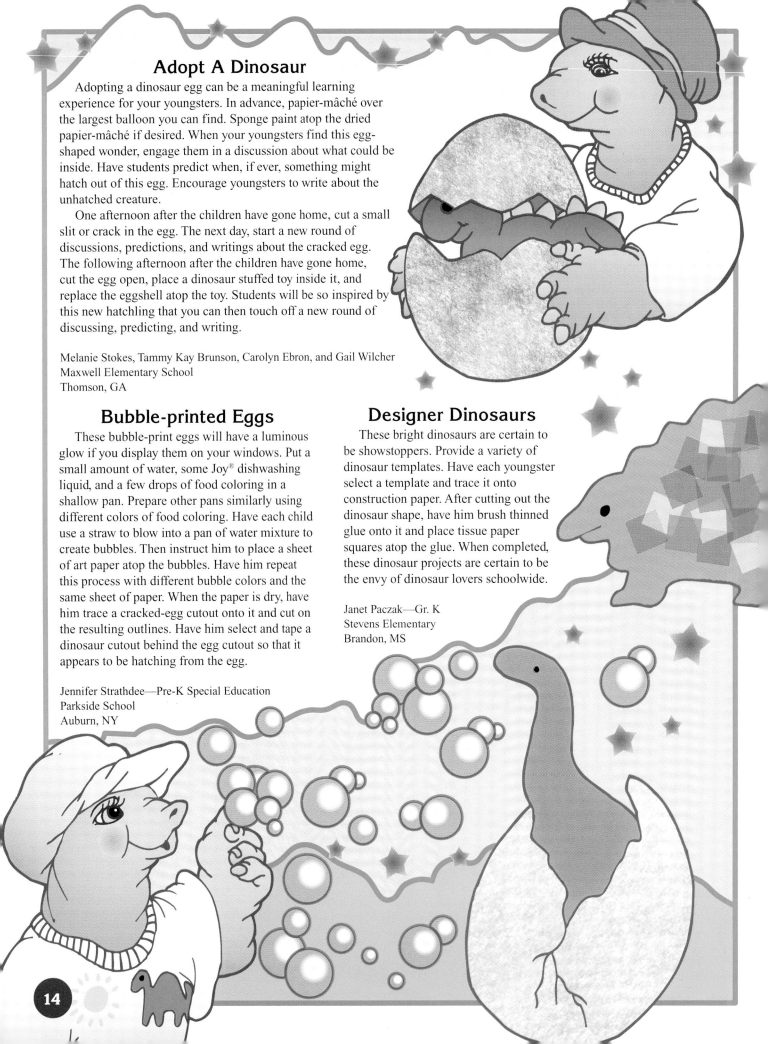

Adopt A Dinosaur

Adopting a dinosaur egg can be a meaningful learning experience for your youngsters. In advance, papier-mâché over the largest balloon you can find. Sponge paint atop the dried papier-mâché if desired. When your youngsters find this egg-shaped wonder, engage them in a discussion about what could be inside. Have students predict when, if ever, something might hatch out of this egg. Encourage youngsters to write about the unhatched creature.

One afternoon after the children have gone home, cut a small slit or crack in the egg. The next day, start a new round of discussions, predictions, and writings about the cracked egg. The following afternoon after the children have gone home, cut the egg open, place a dinosaur stuffed toy inside it, and replace the eggshell atop the toy. Students will be so inspired by this new hatchling that you can then touch off a new round of discussing, predicting, and writing.

Melanie Stokes, Tammy Kay Brunson, Carolyn Ebron, and Gail Wilcher
Maxwell Elementary School
Thomson, GA

Bubble-printed Eggs

These bubble-print eggs will have a luminous glow if you display them on your windows. Put a small amount of water, some Joy® dishwashing liquid, and a few drops of food coloring in a shallow pan. Prepare other pans similarly using different colors of food coloring. Have each child use a straw to blow into a pan of water mixture to create bubbles. Then instruct him to place a sheet of art paper atop the bubbles. Have him repeat this process with different bubble colors and the same sheet of paper. When the paper is dry, have him trace a cracked-egg cutout onto it and cut on the resulting outlines. Have him select and tape a dinosaur cutout behind the egg cutout so that it appears to be hatching from the egg.

Jennifer Strathdee—Pre-K Special Education
Parkside School
Auburn, NY

Designer Dinosaurs

These bright dinosaurs are certain to be showstoppers. Provide a variety of dinosaur templates. Have each youngster select a template and trace it onto construction paper. After cutting out the dinosaur shape, have him brush thinned glue onto it and place tissue paper squares atop the glue. When completed, these dinosaur projects are certain to be the envy of dinosaur lovers schoolwide.

Janet Paczak—Gr. K
Stevens Elementary
Brandon, MS

14

Use with "Dinosaur Duds" on page 10 and activities on pages 23–26.

Pattern

Use with "Dinosaur Duds" on page 10 and activities on pages 23–26.

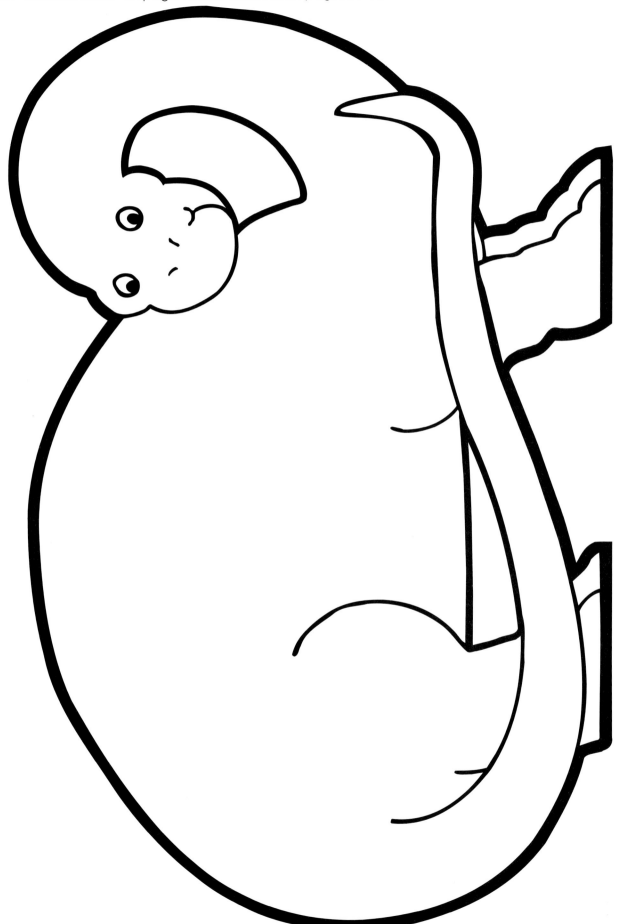

Pattern
Use with "Dinosaur Duds" on page 10 and
activities on pages 23–26.

Pattern
Use with "Counting Eggs" and "Festive Fieldwork" on page 11.

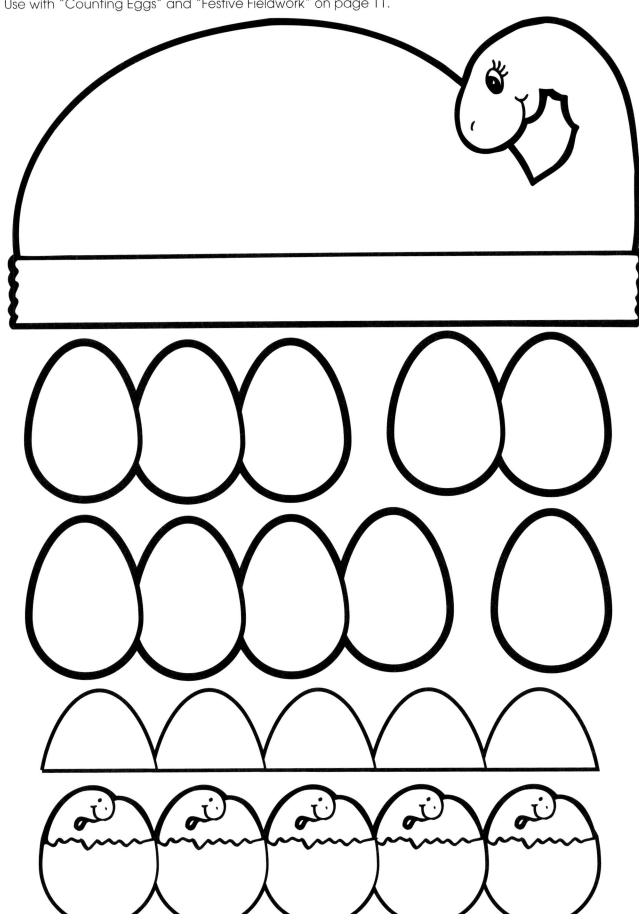

DINO
BINGO

Free

**Bingo Card
Pieces**

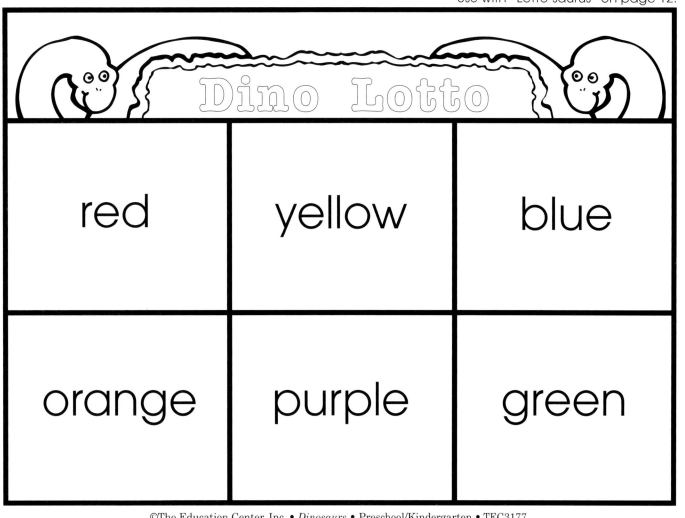

Dino Lotto

red	yellow	blue
orange	purple	green

©The Education Center, Inc. • *Dinosaurs* • Preschool/Kindergarten • TEC3177

Once Upon A Dinosaur's Tale

by Lucia Kemp Henry

Big Old Bones: A Dinosaur Tale
Written by Carol Carrick & Illustrated by Donald Carrick
Published by Clarion Books

Professor Potts is puzzled by the collection of bones he's unearthed. What tremendous creature could they have come from? Your little dinosaur experts will have a fine time fitting together the colorfully drawn clues to help Professor Potts with his dilemma! Read the story a second time, asking students to focus on the antics of the small assistant.

Professor Potts dug and dug until he had enough bones to make more than one dinosaur. Your youngsters can experience similar fun at your classroom sand table. Duplicate each of the dinosaur patterns (pages 15–17) on a different color of construction paper or tagboard. Laminate and cut out each dinosaur before cutting each into four puzzlelike pieces. Bury the pieces in your sand table and provide several digging tools and buckets. Have youngsters work together to find all of the dinosaur puzzle pieces and assemble them to make complete dinosaurs.

Give your youngsters the delightful experience of piecing together dinosaur parts to create a beast similar to the one Professor Potts rigged up. Using an opaque projector, enlarge the patterns on page 28 to fit lengths of bulletin-board paper. Divide your youngsters into five small groups, and give each group one of the enlarged patterns, one color of tempera paint, and several decorative sponges of the same shape. Have each group of students sponge-print their enlarged pattern with tempera paint. When the paint is dry, ask student volunteers to cut out the patterns. Starting with the tail, attach the pieces one by one to a classroom or hallway wall. This big guy is great for holding announcements or giant vocabulary cards.

Count-a-Saurus
Written by Nancy Blumenthal & Illustrated by Robert Jay Kaufman
Published by Four Winds Press

Dinosaur enthusiasts will really get a kick out of this clever counting book. Each number is represented by a different type of prehistoric creature, and each creature is factually described in an "append-a-saurus" at the end of the book.

After reading aloud *Count-a-Saurus,* make an enormous number-line border for your classroom using the dinosaur patterns on pages 15–17. Reproduce the patterns onto construction paper in a variety of colors. Cut out the copies. Trace five-inch numeral outlines onto construction paper. Ask for student volunteers to color and/or cut out each number. Glue the numbers to dinosaur cutouts, sequence the cutouts, and display them in a line around your room. When working with numeration, your dinosaur number line will certainly draw a lot of interest.

Inspired by the rhyme and rhythm of the text of *Count-a-Saurus,* your youngsters will be primed to make up their own version of this counting rhyme. Brainstorm several different dinosaur subjects for the rhymes and focus on a topic or location such as playing on a playground. As students invent each line of verse, write it on chart paper. When the verse is done, provide colorful plastic dinosaur counters, which are available from Lakeshore Learning Materials (1-800-421-5354), or dyed dinosaur-shaped pasta. Have students manipulate the counters or pasta, creating a set to represent each numeral mentioned in their rhyme.

The Tyrannosaurus Game
Written by Steven Kroll & Illustrated by Tomie dePaola
Published by Holiday House

Jimmy starts a little game to perk up a rainy day. But when he selects a Tyrannosaurus rex as the main character, the game becomes a tall tale that grows larger than life.

Offer your students the chance to create an original dinosaur tale. Tape-record each child in turn as he contributes to an add-on story similar in format to the one in the book. When the story is complete, play the tape for your youngsters. Transcribe the recorded story by typing each student's contribution onto a booklet page. Ask students to illustrate the pages before binding the pages into a class booklet. Students may then take turns "reading" the book independently while listening to the tape.

In passing Jimmy's story from one person to another, it gets bigger and more stupendous along the way. Play the game "Gossip" with your youngsters to show that a story can inadvertently evolve as it is retold. Line the students up in single file. Whisper to the first child in line something nonsensical such as, "A Tyrannosaurus was stuck on the stairs." Have him turn to the next person and whisper what he heard. The message is passed along until it reaches the last person in line. This person reports what he heard. Compare the original message to the final one for lots of laughs.

Patrick's Dinosaurs & What Happened To Patrick's Dinosaurs?
Written by Carol Carrick & Illustrated by Donald Carrick
Published by Clarion Books

Patrick has an overactive imagination. His big brother Hank possesses a smattering of scientific expertise. Between the two of them, they manage to conjure up fascinating dinosaur fantasies. Your dinosaur lovers will be enthralled by both of these titles by this wife/husband author/illustrator team.

Encourage your youngsters to imagine a contemporary setting with prehistoric creatures just as Patrick did in *Patrick's Dinosaurs*. Enlarge a triceratops pattern (page 17) onto a bulletin-board background. Have students sponge-paint the dinosaur; then have them draw, color, and cut out contemporary elements such as cars, buses, and people to display alongside the huge horned beast.

In *What Happened To Patrick's Dinosaurs?*, Patrick hypothesized that dinosaurs left Earth in a spaceship and still watch us from the heavens. Discuss this zany theory with your youngsters and use it as a springboard for more imaginative thoughts. Ask them to think of ways the earth must have changed since the dinosaurs were here. What modern circumstances or conveniences might appeal to the dinosaurs, making it possible to lure them back to Earth? After examining the zany possibilities, have student volunteers make pitches touting the luxuries and attractions of this planet in an attempt to lure the dinosaurs back to their original home. Record these statements on videotape or audiotape for playback later.

Dinosaur Bob And His Adventures With The Family Lazardo

Written & Illustrated by William Joyce
Published by Harper & Row, Publishers

It seems as if the dream of every child is to find and befriend a friendly dinosaur. In this case, the benign beast is not only friendly, but can also swim the river Nile, play the trumpet, eat peanut-butter-and-bologna sandwiches, and rescue an underdog baseball team from a perpetual losing streak.

The Lazardo family was quite good at caring for Dinosaur Bob. They gave him plenty of food and played baseball with him. But most of all, they loved him. Have each of your youngsters dictate a sentence describing one way to care for a pet dinosaur. After writing the sentence on a sheet of art paper, have each youngster illustrate his sentence with a drawing of himself caring for a dinosaur in the way mentioned. Bind these pages into a class book titled "Caring For Your Dinosaur."

The Lazardos certainly had many fine traveling adventures with their friend Bob. With your youngsters, discuss the most unusual aspects of their travels with Bob. Ask each of your youngsters to recall a vacation destination he has visited or think of some place he would like to visit. Ask him to imagine that a dinosaur friend accompanies him on his trip. If possible, have each student examine a brochure for his vacation destination to remind him of things he and his dinosaur could do together. Discuss this trip with each child to stimulate thoughts of how this excursion could be different from others due to the presence of the dinosaur. Videotape an interview with each youngster as he "returns home from his trip" wearing or bearing souvenirs. Be sure to ask some of the pros and cons about having a dinosaur for a traveling companion at this particular vacation destination.

Bones, Bones, Dinosaur Bones

Written & Illustrated by Byron Barton
Published by Thomas Y. Crowell

If your youngsters like the idea of poking around in the dirt in search of old dinosaur bones, they'll enjoy this inviting book. Simple text and bright, bold graphics will catch the eyes of your youngsters while simply showing them the exacting science of paleontology.

After reading the story, ask your youngsters to work in small groups to make their own how-to guides for assembling dinosaur bones. Explain that the "how-tos" must be in sequential steps. Have students write four or five steps, basing their ideas on the book. Videotape your little experts dressed as professors as they read or dramatize their creative instructions for dinosaur assembly.

Just as the workers in the book worked together to reconstruct dinosaur skeletons, give your youngsters opportunities to fit together the pieces of dinosaur puzzles. If you are interested in making dinosaur reconstruction into a really big deal, use a fine-tip marker to visually divide a dinosaur pattern (pages 15–17) into several puzzle pieces. Enlarge the dinosaur and trace each puzzle piece design onto tagboard. Laminate and cut out the pieces. Students can work together to assemble this giant floor puzzle.

The Dinosaur Who Lived In My Backyard

Written by B. G. Hennessy & Illustrated by Susan Davis
Published by Viking Kestrel

If we close our eyes and really try, we can imagine a land that has been transformed. We can imagine a land that dinosaurs called home. The child in this story does just that. He imagines that his backyard and neighborhood have been transformed into a world filled with endearing prehistoric pals.

After reading the story, have your youngsters make a dinosaur-inhabited bulletin-board backyard. Cut out colored construction-paper house shapes and staple them to create a border along the bottom of a bulletin board. Have each youngster paint and cut out large newsprint dinosaurs. Trace each of these dinosaurs onto plain newsprint, cut on the outline, and staple this cutout to the back of the painted one, leaving an opening along one side. Stuff the dinosaur with shredded newspaper and staple it closed. Post dinosaurs on the board with the title "Our Backyard Dinosaurs."

You'll be a huge success when you help your youngsters prepare a simple papier-mâché dinosaur. For the dinosaur's form, start with an inflated balloon body. To the balloon, tape toilet-tissue-tube legs, a rolled paper tail, and a paper-towel-tube neck. Wad up a sheet of newspaper and tape it to the paper-towel tube for a head. Have youngsters assist in wrapping the form in papier-mâché. When the papier-mâché is dry, have youngsters paint it with tempera paint. Spray the dinosaur with fixative, if desired. Put this dinosaur in the block corner where it can roam among small plastic figures of people. Encourage students to re-enact the story using these props.

Dinosaur Dream

Written & Illustrated by Dennis Nolan
Published by Macmillan Publishing Company, Inc.

Is it a dream, or is it a living, breathing dinosaur? All Wilbur knows is that he must return the Apatosaurus to its ancient home in time. Beautiful illustrations of a boy and a baby dinosaur bring this fabulous fantasy to life.

I Dreamed About A Dinosaur!
by Jordan

He had a really long neck
saur was green and very
he wore a straw hat.

As young Wilbur discovered, anything is possible in a dream. Use copies of the story starter on page 29 to tuck your youngsters in with original dinosaur dreams. After brainstorming as a group, ask each student to illustrate his own dinosaur dream in the space provided on his copy of the story starter. In the space provided at the bottom of the page, write a student-dictated description of his dinosaur dream. (Glue on a blank sheet of paper if more room is needed.) If desired, staple a rectangle of quilted fabric or flannel along the left margin of the paper to resemble a bed covering. This will cover the dictated writing until folded back.

Gee, wouldn't it be wonderful if each of your youngsters had a dinosaur companion at home? Using the patterns on pages 15–17, this is simple to accomplish. Duplicate the pages on fluorescent or brightly colored paper. Have each youngster choose and cut out a dinosaur before gluing it to a tongue depressor. Ask each youngster to name his dinosaur and copy the name onto the cutout. Using Elmer's® GluColors™, trace over each name. When the glue is dry, students can put on impromptu puppet shows before taking the stick puppets home.

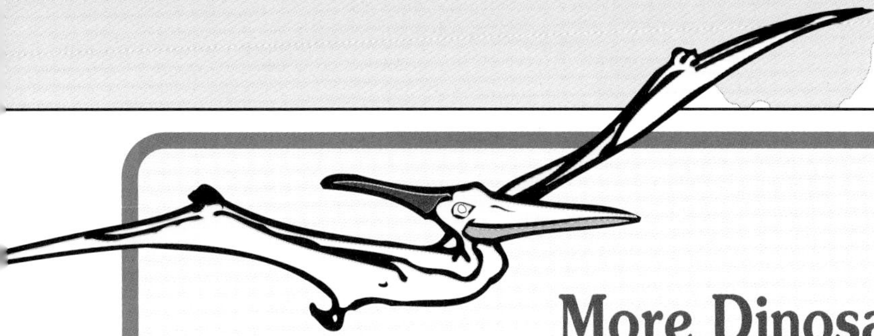

More Dinosaur Tales

The Last Dinosaur
Written by Jim Murphy & Illustrated by Mark Alan Weatherby
Published by Scholatsic Inc.

Prehistoric Pinkerton
Written & Illustrated by Steven Kellogg
Published by Dial Books For Young Readers

How I Captured A Dinosaur
Written by Henry Schwartz & Illustrated by Amy Schwartz
Published by Orchard Books

The Day Of The Dinosaur
Written by Stan & Jan Berenstain & Illustrated by Michael Berenstain
Published by Random House

Whatever Happened To The Dinosaurs?
If The Dinosaurs Came Back
Written & Illustrated by Bernard Most
Published by Harcourt Brace Jovanovich

Tyrone The Horrible
Tyrone The Double Dirty Rotten Cheater
Written & Illustrated by Hans Wilhelm
Published by Scholatic Inc.

Derek The Knitting Dinosaur
Written by Mary Blackwood & Illustrated by Kerry Argent
Published by Carolrhoda Books, Inc.

Dinosaur Bones
Dinosaurs Are Different
Fossils Tell Of Long Ago
My Visit To The Dinosaurs
Written & Illustrated by Aliki
Published by Trophy

T.R. (Tyrannosaurus Rex) & Friends
Written by Rupert Matthews & Illustrated by Tudor Humphries
Published by Discovery Toys

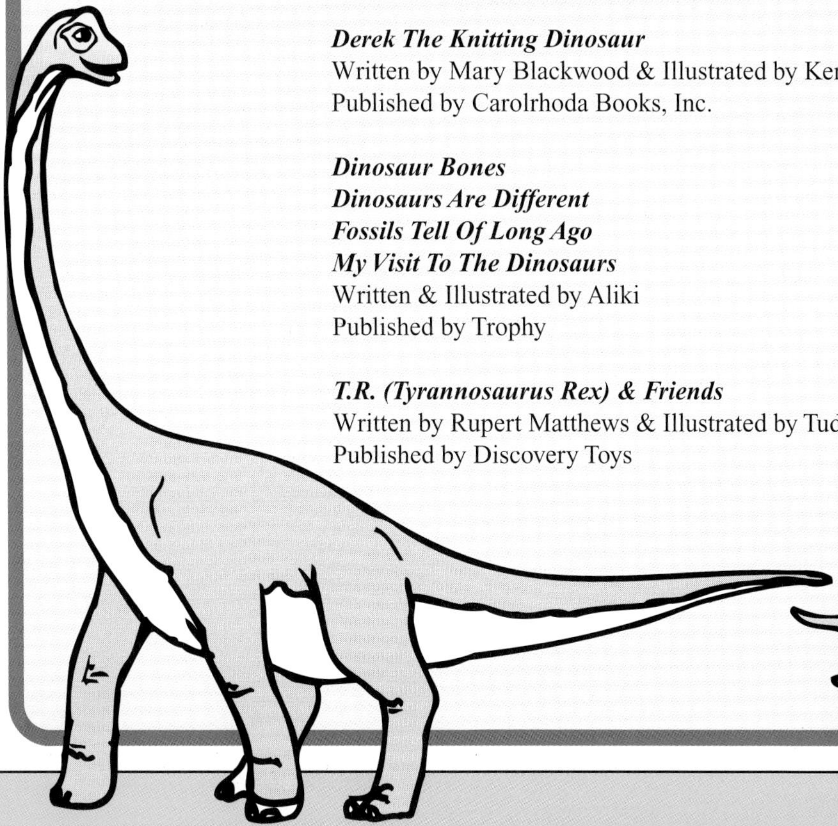

Pattern

Use with the second activity for *Big Old Bones* on page 23.

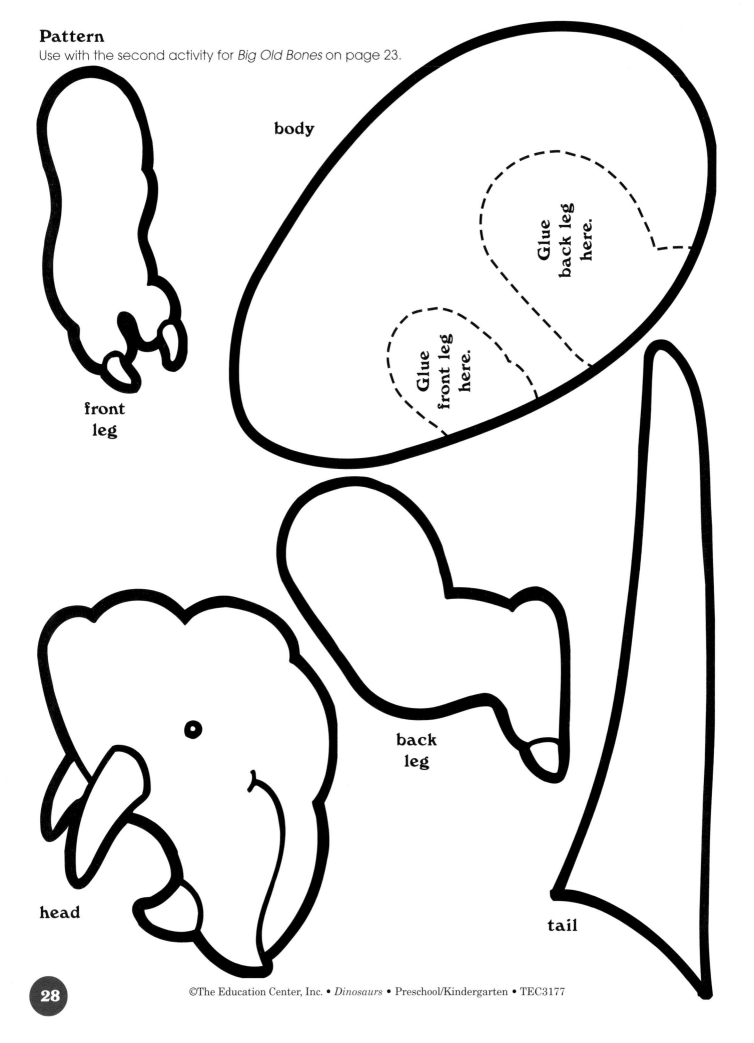

body

Glue back leg here.

Glue front leg here.

front leg

head

back leg

tail

I Dreamed About A Dinosaur!

by _____

The dinosaur

More "Dino-Mite"

Dazzle The Dinosaur

Read aloud Marcus Pfister's *Dazzle The Dinosaur* (North-South Books); then dazzle your little ones with these dandy dinosaurs. Provide each child with several precut, construction-paper dinosaur shapes and Crayola® glitter crayons. Have him color his shapes; then place them between sheets of paper. To create a dazzling effect, rub a warm iron across the paper. Remove the paper. The melted wax and shimmering glitter make these dinosaurs really dazzling!

adapted from an idea by Cheryl Cicioni—Preschool
Kindernook Preschool, Lancaster, PA

Delightful Dinosaurs

Now this is a "dino-mite" art idea that works like magic! Using white crayon, have each child trace a dinosaur pattern (heavily applying the crayon) on white construction paper. If desired, have each student trade papers with a classmate. Then have them brush a thin coat of diluted tempera paint on the papers, and watch the dinosaurs magically appear.

Pat Gaddis—Pre/K
St. Timothy's Methodist Church School, Houston, TX

Dramatic Dinosaur Duds

Knock your little ones' socks off with these exciting dinosaur duds! To make a dinosaur paw, cut the hook side of a strip of self-adhesive Velcro® to match the width of the toe section of a large tube sock. Attach the Velcro® to the top of the sock's toe. Cut out three to five colorful felt triangles—the paw's claws—for each dinosaur paw. For dramatic dinosaur play, encourage a child to select a number of claws to attach to a paw's Velcro®. Then direct him to put his hand and arm into the paw. Roar! These paws help little ones grab onto color recognition, counting, sorting, and more!

Helen Honea—Preschool
Prelude Preschool, Prescott Unified District #1, Prescott, AZ

Dinosaur Ideas • • • • • •

Take a trip to Dinosaur Land! Use bulletin-board paper to create a landscape background. For an interesting 3-D effect, stuff plastic grocery bags behind some of the scenery before completely stapling it to the board. Have each child use art supplies to make an original dinosaur. Help each child staple her dinosaur to just the right place in Dinosaur Land. This also makes a great beginning for some very creative writing!

Debbie Newsome—Gr. K, Dolvin Elementary School, Alpharetta, GA

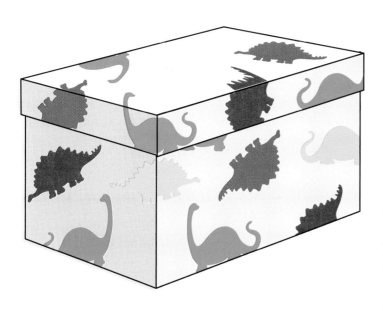

Dinosaur Theme Box

Your youngsters will know they're in for a "dino-mite" day when your substitute teacher hauls out the dinosaur box! Cover a lidded box with dinosaur gift wrap or self-adhesive covering. Fill the box with several days' worth of dinosaur ideas and the materials and resources for carrying them out. Also include the classroom schedules and other information your substitute will need. Your youngsters will appreciate the change of pace and the fun-filled topic. And your substitute will appreciate not having to scramble around looking for supplies.

Ann Marie Lake—Gr. K
Woodland Academy, Ware, MA

Prehistoric Pasta Project!

Here's a hands-on opportunity for your youngsters to create a prehistoric project. Have each student look through magazines, cut out a landscape picture (*National Geographic* magazine is a good resource), and glue his scenic picture to a sheet of construction paper. Then have him glue dinosaur-shaped pasta to the picture. Dinosaurs in their habitat!

Carol Hargett, Kinderhaus III, Fairborn, OH

Designer Dinos

Dinosaurs are always a hot topic. So encourage your youngsters to get creative about dinosaurs. To make a designer dinosaur, begin by drawing a large dinosaur shape on a sheet of construction paper. Cut out the design and glue it to a sheet of black construction paper. (Another alternative is to sponge print a dinosaur shape onto the black paper, rather than gluing it.) Use cotton balls, yarn, colored sand, glitter, paint pens, colored pasta, tissue paper, aquarium rocks, and colored popcorn to make your dinosaur distinctively different. Looks like it's time for a private showing. The dino designs are complete!

Adetrice Garrett Patterson—Gr. K
Inverness Elementary School, Birmingham, AL

Dinosaurs, Dinosaurs

Here's a book your preschool paleontologists are sure to dig! During storytime share *Dinosaurs, Dinosaurs* by Byron Barton (HarperCollins Children's Books). After carefully viewing the pictures, have youngsters suggest a list of ways that the dinosaurs described in the book are different. As a challenge, have them help you make a list of ways that the dinosaurs are alike.

As a creative story extension, stock an art center with different colors of paint poured into tins, various colors of construction paper, pencils, scissors, and dinosaur-shaped cookie cutters. Encourage each child to dip several different cookie cutters into the paint and press them onto a sheet of paper. Encourage him to describe ways that his dinosaur prints are alike and different. Or suggest that he trace the cutters onto a sheet of paper and cut on the resulting outlines. Later mount the shapes on craft sticks to create puppets.

If making these prehistoric prints or puppets has created big appetites, serve several snacks suitable for plant eaters and meat eaters alike. For the herbivores, prepare plates of lettuce and raw vegetables with a tasty dip. To satisfy the carnivores, serve hot dogs for dipping in chili.

Diane DiMarco—Three- And Four-Year-Olds
Country Kids Preschool, Groton, MA

Top-Notch Dinosaur

These decorative dinosaurs are sure to razzle-dazzle even the youngest of dinoenthusiasts! Cut the outline shape of a triceratops dinosaur from half a sheet of white poster board. Using two different colors of paint, sponge-paint the dinosaur shape. Set the painted shape aside to dry. Cut a coffee filter in half. Using a piece of colored chalk that matches one of the colors of paint, gently rub the flat side of the chalk over the ridges of the coffee-filter half. To adhere the chalk to the filter, spray it with hairspray. Glue the filter half to the neck, a wiggle eye to the head, and spiral-shaped pasta to each of the dinosaur's horns. These triceratops really are tops!

Janine Nordland—Preschool, Owatonna, MN

A "Dino" Search

Now here's a real dinosaur hunt! Draw or trace several different types of dinosaurs on separate sheets of paper. Reproduce each different dinosaur picture several times on the same color of construction paper; then laminate the sheets, if desired. Provide each child with one sheet and have him examine his dinosaur picture. Then have each student move to a different area of the room and hold up his picture. Instruct each student to find other students with corresponding dinosaur pictures and to stand together in a group. When every child has found the other children with pictures that match his own, gather the groups back to the circle to examine each group's dinosaurs and to celebrate a successful dinosaur search.

June Moss—Pre-K
Sunbeams And Rainbows Pre-School, Elmhurst, IL

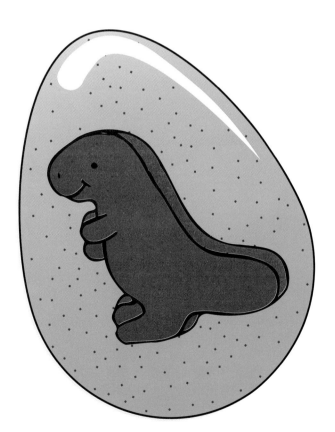

Dinosaur Treats

If you are fortunate enough to have a Jell-O® Egg Jigglers® mold, you can surprise your little ones with this prehistoric egg snack. Using green Jell-O®, follow the package directions to prepare Jell-O® Jigglers®. Stir cinnamon into the mixture to create a speckled effect. Place a dinosaur-shaped fruit snack in each egg shape before closing it. Then pour the Jell-O® in the mold. Refrigerate the eggs. Serve the eggs at snacktime. Your children will be delighted to find a baby dinosaur nestled inside their eggs!

Christine T. Dise—Four-Year-Olds
Pottstown YMCA Childcare, Pottstown, PA

Counting Dinos

Nancy Blumenthal's *Count-A-Saurus* (Four Winds Press) is a great book to reinforce counting skills and introduce facts about prehistoric creatures. While reading the book, point to each dinosaur on the page as students count orally. After reading it, program each of ten large sheets of construction paper with a numeral and number word from one to ten. Assign each sheet of paper to a pair of students or a small group. Using the book as a reference, have youngsters draw and color the appropriate number of dinosaurs on their sheet. Place the pages between construction-paper covers; then bind the pages together. Display the book in a center with dinosaur counters or dinosaur-shaped pasta. Encourage students to manipulate the counters or pasta, creating a set to represent each numeral in the book. Now that's a "dino-mite" idea!

Andrea Troisi—Librarian
LaSalle Middle School, Niagara Falls, NY

The "Dino-Pokey"

What has claws, sharp teeth, big feet, and a long tail? A preschooler pretending to be a dinosaur! Ask all of your prehistoric preschoolers to form a group circle. Then encourage them to sing this song (to the tune of "The Hokey Pokey") and move along!

Put your claws in. Put your claws out.
Put your claws in and scratch them all about.
Do the "dino-pokey" and turn yourself around.
That's what it's all about!

Put your teeth in...chomp them all about.

Put your feet in...stomp them all about.

Put your tail in...wag it all about.

Diane DiMarco—Three- And Four-Year-Olds
Country Kids Preschool, Groton, MA

grrr

Tracking Dinosaurs

The imaginations of your dinosaur enthusiasts are sure to roam about in this art center. Cut sponges into several sizes of dinosaur footprint shapes. Provide shallow bowls, each of which contains a set of paper towels that have been soaked with a color of paint. A child makes a dinosaur footprint by dipping the sponge (dinosaur foot) into a color of paint and then repeatedly pressing the sponge onto a piece of art paper. For added fun, provide a long sheet of butcher paper on which children can really "make tracks!"

Janet Paczak—Gr. K, Stevens Elementary, Brandon, MS

Dinosaur Eggs

Delight youngsters with these delectable dinosaur eggs. Combine the following ingredients in a large bowl:

     1/2 cup peanut butter
     1/2 cup honey
     1 cup powdered milk
     1/2 cup raisins
     1/2 cup GRAPE-NUTS® cereal

Knead the mixture thoroughly; then roll into egg shapes. "Dino-licious!"

Kimberle Byrd, Wyoming, MI

Fossil Math

Transform your math center into a paleontologist's delight! Decorate the center area with toy dinosaurs. From white poster board, cut shapes of varying lengths and widths to represent bones or fossils. (Shape bones from sculptor's clay, if available, and let them dry for a week before using.) Provide rulers and tape measures for youngsters' use in measuring each bone. What a blast from the past!

Janet Paczak

Reproducible Activities...

from **Teacher's Helper**® magazine

Patrick's Dinosaurs

Clarion Books ©1983 illustrated by Donald Carrick

How To Use Page 39

Review the story, *Patrick's Dinosaurs* by Carol Carrick, with your children. In this delightful story, Patrick imagines dinosaurs throughout his town. Help children recall where Patrick imagined he saw the dinosaurs in the story. Children should color those pictures on the worksheet that show where Patrick imagined seeing dinosaurs. (Hint: The flying reptile and the giant swimming turtle are not pictures from the story.) For more ideas to use with *Patrick's Dinosaurs* and *What Happened To Patrick's Dinosaurs?* see page 24.

Finished Sample

Patrick Imagines

Think and color.

GROCERY

An Imaginary Trip

Patrick imagines dinosaurs in his town.

Patrick can imagine he is in Dinosaur Land.
✏️ Draw a picture of what he can imagine.

If I could have any big, tremendous pet,

I'd wish for a dinosaur, the biggest pet yet!

I'd like a dinosaur for a pet because

by _____

...In The Time Of Dinosaurs...

Background For The Teacher

Dinosaurs were present during the Triassic, Jurassic, and Cretaceous periods in the earth's history. These three periods comprise the Mesozoic Era, 225 to 64 million years ago. Early humans did not appear on earth until about 2 to 3 million years ago. Obviously, "cavemen" never did battle with ferocious dinosaurs!

How To Use Page 43

1. Read the basic concept sentences at the top of the worksheet. Allow discussion to help emphasize that movies or television shows the children may have seen showing dinosaurs and people living at the same time are fictitious.

2. Help the children identify the six pictures at the bottom of the page. As you identify the pictures, discuss whether or not one might have seen each thing in the time of dinosaurs. Briefly discuss that some dinosaurs ate plants and some ate meat to justify the picture of the plant.

3. The children should color only those pictures that would have been seen in the time of the dinosaurs. *(Obviously, the "cave child" and teepee are not to be colored since man came about 60 million years after dinosaurs were gone!)*

Finished Sample

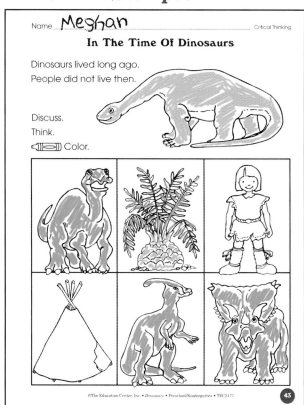

In The Time Of Dinosaurs

Dinosaurs lived long ago.

People did not live then.

Discuss.

Think.

Color.

43

...In The Time Of Dinosaurs...

Background For The Teacher
Dinosaur Sizes

Today, when we think of dinosaurs, we think of towering giants like Tyrannosaurus rex (18 feet tall, 46 feet long) and Diplodocus (88 feet long). Scientists have discovered that dinosaurs existed in a wide range of sizes. Like modern animals, dinosaurs fit into a wide variety of environmental niches, with sizes to match.

Anchisaurus was small—about eight feet long—but only as tall an an adult human's knee. It was light in weight and most likely agile in order to avoid larger predators. It probably ate plants.

Velociraptor was about six feet tall. It was most likely a swift carnivore, preying on other dinosaurs. Some believe that, because of its small size, it may have hunted in groups, like wolves.

Ceratosaurus was a midsized dinosaur—20 feet long—much taller than a man, but shorter than a Tyrannosaurus. It was a carnivore with massive jaws and sharp, curved teeth. It may have been quite agile and, being large, was probably a solitary hunter.

How To Use Page 45

1. Share the facts above about each dinosaur on the worksheet. Have each child identify the dinosaur as you discuss it. Then have him cut out the dinosaur and glue it in the appropriate box.

2. As a follow-up, enlarge the dinosaurs; then attach each one to the top of a language experience chart. Draw a vertical column for each dinosaur. Remind the children of the sizes of these particular dinosaurs, and encourage them to think of things they know of that are the same size. List the suggestions under each dinosaur. For example, Velociraptor was as big as a man, or perhaps as tall as the slide on the playground.

Finished Sample

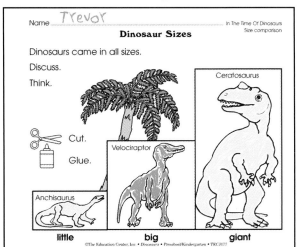

44

Name _____

Dinosaur Sizes

Dinosaurs came in all sizes.

Discuss.

Think.

Cut.

Glue.

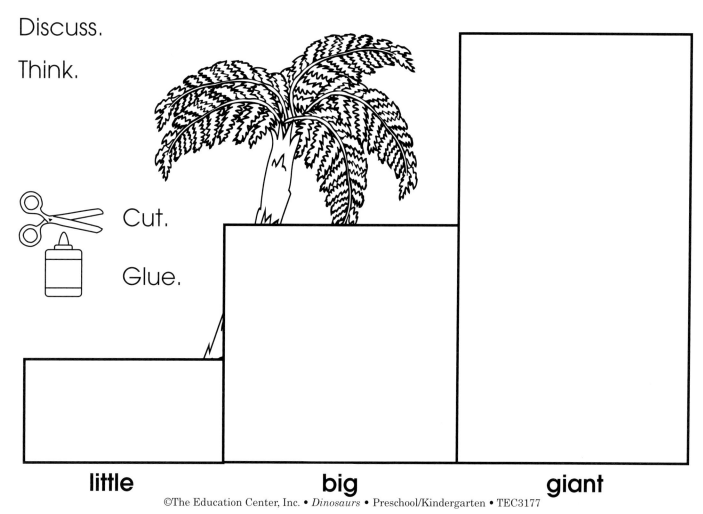

little   big   giant

©The Education Center, Inc. • *Dinosaurs* • Preschool/Kindergarten • TEC3177

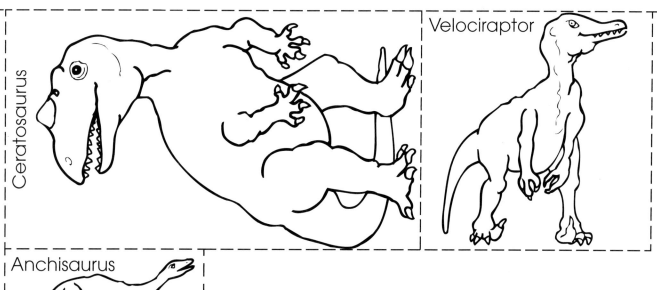

Ceratosaurus

Velociraptor

Anchisaurus

45

...In The Time Of Dinosaurs.

Background For The Teacher
Dinosaur Bones

How does a scientist find a dinosaur? The first step is to look in deposits of sedimentary rock from the Mesozoic Era. Scientists must look in exposed deposits of clays, limestones, sandstones, and mudstones. Some dinosaur skeletons are found during purposeful expeditions. Others are discovered accidentally by miners, road excavation crews, and even farmers.

The excavation of a dinosaur skeleton is a slow and painstaking process. Fossil skeletons must be labeled, sketched, and photographed before being removed from the rock. Soil and rock are removed carefully from around the fossil mass. The skeleton must be cut into moveable sizes and then transported to the laboratory.

In the lab, the fossil bones are carefully cleaned and hardened using intricate tools and chemicals. Scientists sometimes use skeleton models of modern birds and animals to aid in reconstruction of dinosaur skeletons. There are many theories as to how the skeleton of even one species may look. For more specific and fascinating reading, refer to the book *The Illustrated Encyclopedia Of Dinosaurs* by Dr. David Norman.

The last step in finding a dinosaur is to "clothe" it in muscles and skin, making an illustrated and a three-dimensional model. By studying the bones, scientists can imagine the attachments, type, size, and shape of the muscles and their complementary covering.

How To Use Page 47

1. Read the concept sentences at the top of the worksheet. Share some of the information in the background above.
2. Call attention to the gray areas of the dinosaur skeleton on the worksheet. Explain that these are areas in which the children must help the scientist find the correct bones to complete the dinosaur. Allow the children to cut out the bone shapes at the bottom of the page, find the corresponding spaces, and then glue them in place.
3. Remind the children that the last step for the scientist is to "clothe" the dinosaur in muscle and skin to show how the dinosaur might have looked. In the empty box on the right, the children may draw a picture of what the dinosaur whose skeleton appears in the left box might have looked like.

Dino Bones

How do we know about dinosaurs?

We find dinosaur bones.

The bones can make a skeleton.

Discuss.

Think.

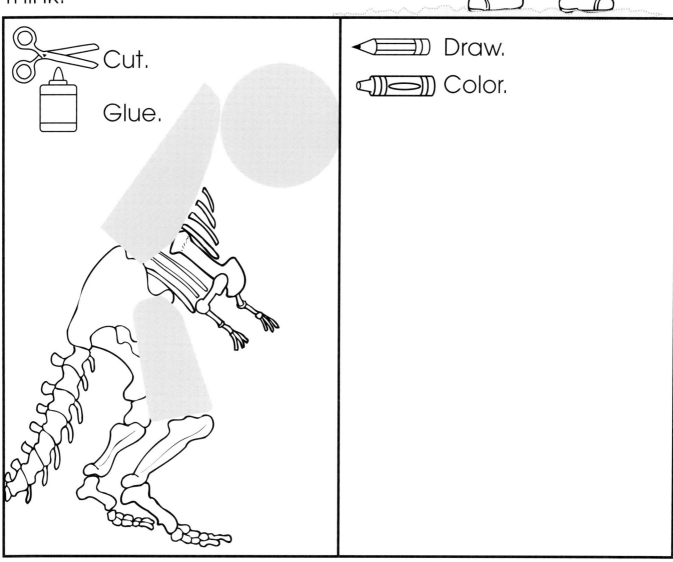

Cut.

Glue.

Draw.

Color.

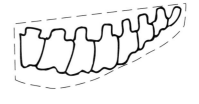

Dino Tracks

Read the words.

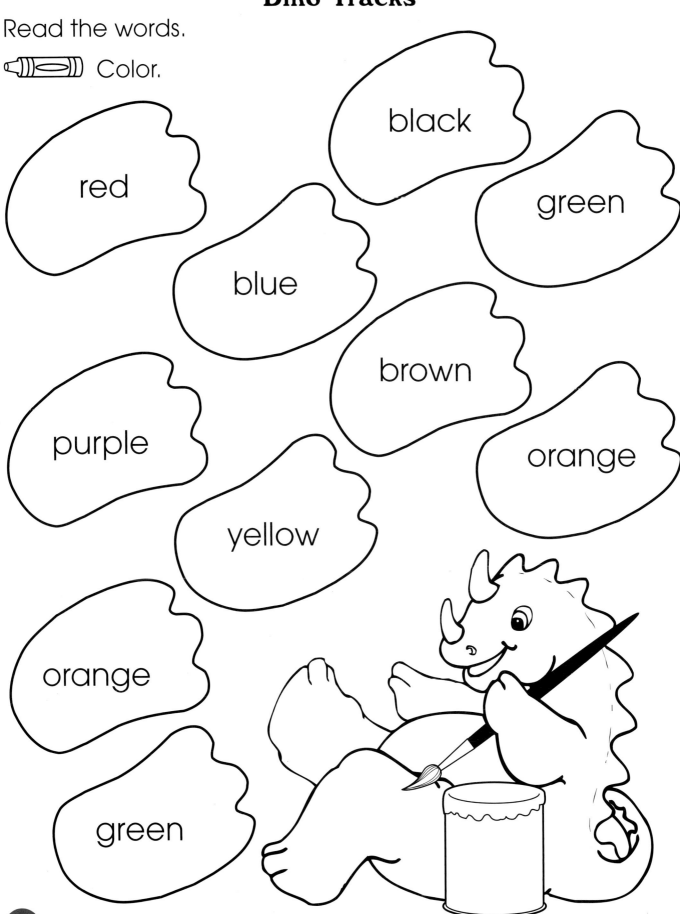 Color.

black

red

green

blue

brown

purple

orange

yellow

orange

green

©The Education Center, Inc. • *Dinosaurs* • Preschool/Kindergarten • TEC3177